ANIMAL FAMILIES
Penguins

General Editor
Tim Harris

WAYLAND

WAYLAND

This edition published in 2014 by Wayland

Copyright © 2014 Brown Bear Books Ltd.

Wayland
Hachette Children's Books
338 Euston Road
London NW1 3BH

Wayland Australia
Level 17/207 Kent Street
Sydney, NSW 2000

All Rights Reserved.

Brown Bear Books Ltd.
First Floor
9–17 St. Albans Place
London
N1 0NX

Managing Editor: Tim Harris
Designer: Lynne Lennon
Picture Manager: Sophie Mortimer
Art Director: Jeni Child
Production Director: Alastair Gourlay
Editorial Director: Lindsey Lowe
Children's Publisher: Anne O'Daly

ISBN: 978-0-7502-8454-7

Printed in China

10 9 8 7 6 5 4 3 2 1

Wayland is a division of Hachette Children's Books,
an Hachette UK company.
www.hachette.co.uk

Websites
The website addresses (URLs) included in this book were valid at the time of going to press. However, because of the nature of the internet, it is possible that some addresses may have changed, or sites may have changed or closed down since publication. While the author and publisher regret any inconvenience this may cause the readers, no responsibility for any such changes can be accepted by either the author or the publisher.

Contents

Introduction

Penguins are among the most familiar and best loved of any wild birds. Some live in Antarctica, the world's coldest continent.

There are 17 different species (types) of penguins, including the king penguin, emperor penguin, Adélie penguin and fairy penguin. Some penguins are found close to the equator, the imaginary line that runs around the middle of Earth. Far more live in the icy wastes of Antarctica. Penguins cannot fly and they waddle clumsily on land. However, they are expert swimmers. In short bursts they can 'fly' through the water at 32 kilometres per hour (20 mph).

⬙ **Penguins are clumsy walkers. Belly sliding is often a quicker way to move around on ice and snow!**

Penguins are very sociable birds. That means they do most things in groups, especially in the breeding season. A place where large numbers of penguins breed is called a colony, or rookery. Some colonies are huge: more than two million macaroni penguins breed on one small island.

Questions and answers

Why do penguins get together in these enormous colonies? And why do they do other things in groups? In this book you will find the answers to these questions. You will also discover more about these fascinating birds, including where they live and how they bring up their chicks.

Macaroni penguins are named after their yellow or orange crests.

What's in a name?

Some types of penguins have been given more than one common name. For example, the chinstrap penguin is also sometimes known as the ringed penguin or the bearded penguin. This can become very confusing.

To simplify matters, scientists give all animals a scientific name, which never changes. For example, the chinstrap penguin's scientific name is *Pygoscelis antarctica*.

Safety in numbers

Penguins live in groups for one main reason – there is safety in numbers. A group of penguins is more likely to see an enemy than a lone bird is.

Penguins breed in colonies because this gives their chicks a better chance of survival. Penguin groups have no real social structure. In many ways they are like shoals of fish – every bird is equal, and there are no leaders. But unlike fish, penguins have times when they need their own space. Penguins nesting in colonies are almost always spread out evenly, out of pecking reach of one another.

Time for a change

Once a year every penguin must change its feathers. This change is called moulting. A moult takes between two and six weeks. It starts from several weeks to several months after the breeding season. Moulting penguins cannot swim or hunt for fish, so they fatten themselves up as much as they can before the process begins.

◔ A penguin looks scruffy when it is moulting its old feathers, but it has to moult because its feathers suffer from wear and tear.

A colony of king penguins. Penguins usually establish their colonies by the coast so they do not have to travel long distances from the sea with food for their chicks.

Huddling together for warmth

A few penguins live in groups for more than just protection from predators (animals that hunt and kill them). Male emperor penguins huddle together during the freezing Antarctic winters to keep themselves warm. Some scientists also think that penguins may hunt better in groups than on their own. This is a difficult thing to prove, though.

Diving for fish

Penguins live mainly on a diet of fish and krill, tiny shrimp-like creatures that often swarm in huge numbers. Larger penguins also dive for squid.

Penguins are very good at hunting their slippery prey. They are fast, agile swimmers and can twist and turn to follow the movements of fleeing shoals of fish. Penguins' eyes see well underwater. Some penguins have better vision in the water than on dry land.

⬆ **Gentoo penguins leap out of the water and bellyflop on the ice after a successful fishing trip.**

Far and deep

Some penguins swim long distances to get food. Emperor penguins are the greatest travellers. They may stay at sea for a month at a time and travel 1,500 kilometres (950 miles) from their breeding grounds in search of food. They also perform some truly remarkable dives. One emperor penguin was recorded diving to 535 metres (1,752 feet) below the surface of the water.

⬆ Emperor penguins can dive to great depths and stay under water for up to 18 minutes.

Penguins do not have teeth, but they do have tough spikes on their tongue and the roof of the mouth. These spikes are ideal for grasping slippery fish.

Fitting the bill

King and emperor penguins mainly hunt squid, and they have long, pincer-like beaks to snap up their long-bodied, fast-moving prey. Smaller penguins that eat more krill or fish have shorter, stubbier bills.

Penguins can eat very large quantities of food. One Magellanic penguin was found to have eaten almost 4 kilograms (9 lbs) of squid in a single hunt. On the other hand, penguins are very good at surviving when there is little food. When they are moulting, and so unable to hunt, most species of penguin can survive for weeks on end without any food.

Time to breed

With the exception of one species, penguins breed once a year. Most gather at their nesting colonies in late spring to mate and lay their eggs.

Most penguins rear their young so they are ready to swim by the summer. A few species do things differently, however. Emperor penguins incubate their eggs (sit on them to keep them warm) through the winter. Those that live farther north, for example macaroni penguins, start breeding in the middle of winter so that their chicks are ready to go to sea in late spring. The real odd one out is the king penguin. Its chicks take up to

To build or not

Most penguins face a big problem when it comes to building a nest – the lack of suitable building materials. Some get around this by not making a nest at all. King and emperor penguins balance their eggs on their feet.

The alternative is to build a nest from pebbles or to lay eggs on the bare ground. Magellanic penguins (left) build their nests from grass. But because penguins cannot fly, the nest material has to be found nearby.

➡ **Two king penguins touch their beaks together and make friends.**

16 months to grow, so the adults can only breed twice every three years at the most.

Chaos in the colony

The breeding season is a noisy, bustling time for all penguins. Males usually arrive at the colony first and set about finding the place where they nested the year before.

First-time breeders have to grab an empty site or settle on the edge of the colony. Male penguins try to attract females by calling loudly. Eventually almost all of the males will find a mate.

⬇ **King penguins at a colony on the island of South Georgia. Some king penguins pair up in spring and others in summer.**

Egg laying and incubation

Soon after she has paired up and mated, a female penguin lays her eggs. King and emperor penguins lay a single egg. All other penguins lay two.

Penguins lay very small eggs for their body size. The emperor penguin lays the smallest egg of any bird in proportion to its bodyweight. Its egg tips the scales at just 1.4 per cent of the bird's weight.

Although they are small, penguin eggs are very strong. They have super-thick eggshells. This is just as well because the parents are very clumsy on land. Weak eggs would not last long in colonies crowded with clumsy adults.

With the exception of emperor penguins, both parents take turns at incubating the eggs. The smallest penguins incubate, or brood, the

Female gentoo penguins lay two eggs. The parents share incubation duties, changing over several times a day.

eggs for the shortest time. Fairy penguins spend just 33 days sitting before their eggs hatch, whereas macaroni penguins incubate for 36 days. Large king penguins brood for 55 days and emperor penguins brood for the longest time – 64 days.

Cradle snatchers

Nesting penguins have to protect their eggs from thieves. Gulls and other scavenging seabirds, such as skuas and sheathbills, regularly patrol penguin colonies looking for unguarded eggs to eat. Small chicks are also vulnerable if they are not watched carefully.

Male emperor penguins do not eat while they are incubating their egg. They may lose half their body weight during this time.

A long incubation

Emperor penguins have a really tough time during incubation. While most penguin species spend a few weeks keeping their eggs warm before they hatch, emperors do this for more than two months. They incubate during the sunless Antarctic winter, when temperatures can drop as low as −60°C (−76°F). Only the male emperor penguins incubate their single egg.

Bringing up chicks

Penguin chicks chip through the eggshell with the help of an egg tooth, a short spike on the end of the beak. The egg tooth drops off soon after hatching.

Penguin chicks hatch from the egg already covered in a fine coat of downy feathers. The chicks are hungry from the moment they arrive in the outside world. Luckily, most emerge to find a ready-made meal of half-digested fish, krill or squid waiting for them. The parents drop balls of food on

⊘ **A gentoo penguin bends over to check that its chick is warm enough.**

➔ **An emperor penguin chick keeps warm by snuggling up against its parent.**

the egg as it is hatching. In most species, both parents share feeding and caring duties once the chicks have hatched.

Busy parents

One parent keeps the chick or chicks warm while the other searches for food. The hunter returns to cough up its catch for the chick and take over babysitting duties. Then the other parent goes off to hunt for more food.

Most penguins lay two eggs, but usually only one chick survives. The second usually starves to death within two weeks of hatching. The survivor is fed until it is ready to take to the water. This happens at any time from 50 days.

Coughing up food

Most penguins catch their food far out at sea, so bringing it back for their chicks is not a simple matter. Rather than risk losing their catch on the way home, they swallow it. When an adult penguin returns from a fishing trip, the young bird reaches into its parent's throat, forcing it to regurgitate, or cough up, the food.

Growing bigger

The chicks rely on their parents until they have grown their waterproof feathers. For most penguin species, this takes at least two months.

Chicks are kept under constant guard for the first few weeks of their lives. Even in the Antarctic there are plenty of predators (hunters) waiting to take advantage of a helpless baby on its own. By the time they are about four weeks old, most chicks start exploring the area around them.

Safety in numbers

Not long after that, their parents start to leave them on their own. They continue to feed their young during this 'post-guarding stage'. During this time many baby penguins find safety in numbers. While their parents are away fishing, the chicks of king, emperor, Adélie, chinstrap, gentoo and crested

→ A gentoo penguin chick chases its parent for food. Gentoo parents dive underwater up to 450 times a day to look for food for the young penguins.

penguins gather in groups known as crèches. The chicks are less likely to be snatched by predators. In very cold weather chicks may also huddle together to stay warm. When they are between two and four months old, the parents abandon the chicks. By this time most have started to lose their fluffy coats and show their adult plumage. They are usually well stocked with fat to help them survive while they learn how to catch fish for themselves.

King penguin chicks have a fluffy brown coat of down to keep them warm.

Late developers

While most penguins stay as chicks for just a few months, the king penguin makes a marathon of it. King penguins are not ready to go to sea until they are 10 to 13 months old – almost four times older than most others.

Streamlined swimmers

Penguins are amazing swimming machines. Their tightly packed feathers form a smooth covering. The water does not slow them down as they swim.

The penguin's body is perfect for moving through water. Its streamlined shape is similar to that of aquatic (water-living) mammals such as seals, dolphins and whales. When a penguin is hunting, it makes its body even more streamlined by pulling its head into its shoulders and holding its feet tight against the body.

'Flying' through the water

Penguins have perhaps the most unusual wings of any bird. While most birds' wings are ideal for flight, penguins' wings are perfect for swimming. Penguins swim by flapping their flattened wings – or flippers – up and down so that they look like they are flying through the water. The wing bones are fused together to make the flippers stiff and strong.

⊙ **A penguin's wings are of little use once the bird is out of the water.**

Foot notes

Penguins' feet sit far back on their bodies, making walking difficult. However, when the birds are in water their feet help steer them. The blood vessels in penguins' feet lie close together. Cold blood coming back from the ends of the toes is warmed by hot blood travelling into the feet from the body. This helps them stay warm.

Penguins have webs of skin between their toes. The webs help the feet push the birds quickly through water.

Ancient and modern penguins

Penguins have been swimming in the ocean for a very long time. People who study rocks have found penguin fossils that are about 60 million years old.

Scientists think that penguins may have been alive when the last dinosaurs were roaming Earth. At the same time as the dinosaurs became extinct, so did the giant reptiles that once lived in the oceans. This meant there was a lot of food in the sea that penguins could eat.

People think that, between 40 million and 25 million years ago, there were more penguins than there are now – at least 40 types, compared with just 17 today. Half of

Imagine coming face to face with the giant *Anthropornis nordenskjoeldi*. This ancient penguin is known only from its fossil remains.

A group of Magellanic penguins waddles across a beach. They are tiny compared with some of the ancient penguin species.

➲ An albatross glides over the Southern Ocean. Albatrosses fly long distances in search of small fish and other sea creatures.

Flying cousins

The closest living relatives of penguins include the albatrosses. These are some of the biggest flying birds alive today. Albatrosses glide great distances over the oceans in search of fish to eat. The wandering albatross has the largest wingspan of any bird. Its wings are 3.6 metres (11 feet) from one wingtip to the other.

those species were bigger than the emperor penguin, which is the biggest penguin alive today. One of them – called *Anthropornis nordenskjoeldi* – stood as tall as a man and may have weighed as much as 135 kilograms (300 lbs).

Penguins versus dolphins

Penguins are believed to have been the top hunters in the oceans for millions of years. Their reign may have been ended by the dolphins and toothed whales. These water-living mammals became more common 20 to 15 million years ago. The larger penguins may not have been able to compete with them for fish, so they eventually died out.

Enemies all around

Wherever they live, penguins are successful hunters of fish. But penguins themselves are eaten by many larger predators.

In the cold Antarctic waters almost 50 per cent of a leopard seal's diet consists of penguins. They mostly attack Adélie, chinstrap, gentoo and rockhopper penguins. Other seals and sea lions also count penguins among their prey. Perhaps the most fearsome penguin predator of all is the killer whale.

Pods (groups) of killer whales often swim offshore from penguin colonies, waiting to pluck the snack-sized birds from the water.

Airborne killers

Adult penguins have few natural predators outside the sea. Most species nest on remote islands where there are few, if any, mammals. Young penguins and eggs are not so lucky. Penguin colonies are often plagued by airborne killers, such as skuas, giant petrels and sheathbills. These large seabirds are unable to take adults, but they can kill lots of the penguin chicks.

⬆ Sometimes a leopard seal will lie in wait near the shore to grab penguins as they try to leave the water.

Enemy number one

In Antarctic waters the leopard seal is the terror of the sea. These seals hunt penguins in a number of ways. Sometimes they follow the shadow of a bird as it walks on thin ice, smashing through to grab it before it knows what has happened. Sometimes they leap from the sea onto chunks of ice to snatch penguins.

⬅ Killer whales, or orcas, often grab and swallow adult penguins.

Homes in unlikely places

Penguins seem to go with Antarctica like polar bears with the Arctic. But in fact, some penguin species never go near Antarctic waters.

Emperor penguins are hardly ever seen outside the Antarctic, and Adélie penguins live mostly in the cold waters surrounding the southern continent. Chinstrap and gentoo penguins nest on Antarctica and its surrounding islands, but they are also found farther north.

Forest penguins

The remainder of the 17 species nest away from Antarctica. Some breed on the shores of South America and its offshore islands. Others have colonies on the shores of New Zealand and Australia.

The Fjordland penguin has perhaps the strangest nesting places of any species. It brings up its chicks in the cool, wet forests of islands off south-western New Zealand.

Galápagos penguins live on the Galápagos Islands. The islands are thousands of kilometres from icy Antarctica.

⬆ **Yellow-eyed penguins live on the coast of New Zealand's South Island.**

Penguins on the equator

The most northerly penguins of all live in the Galápagos Islands, a group of islands in the Pacific Ocean that straddles the equator. Galápagos penguins eat the fish that swim in the nutrient-rich Cromwell Current. This washes around the islands.

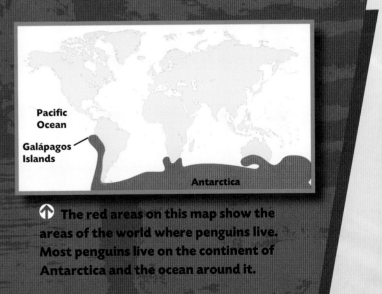

Pacific Ocean

Galápagos Islands

Antarctica

⬆ The red areas on this map show the areas of the world where penguins live. Most penguins live on the continent of Antarctica and the ocean around it.

Never far from the ocean

People usually picture penguins in frozen wastes or on the rocky coasts where most of them breed. But a penguin's real habitat is the open ocean.

The reason that penguins are so clumsy and comical on land is that their bodies are adapted for a life in the water. Watching them swim makes it clear where they are most at home. Most penguins can be found in coastal and oceanic waters south of South America, South Africa, Australia and New Zealand. A few species are seen much farther north. And, as we have already seen, one species – the Galápagos penguin – lives right on the equator.

Closer to water

Wherever penguins are found on land, they are never very far from the sea. Even the male emperor penguins

⊙ **This emperor penguin is standing on a shelf of ice on a frozen part of the Weddell Sea in Antarctica.**

that spend the winter far from the water's edge are closer to the ocean than they realise. In winter much of the ocean around Antarctica freezes, and the 'land' that the emperors spend months incubating their eggs on is actually a shelf of ice floating on the seawater underneath.

King penguins where they are most at home – in the ocean. Places where there is lots of food in the water attract crowds of hungry penguins.

Going underground

Galápagos, jackass, Humboldt, Magellanic and fairy penguins have an added element to their life on land. As well as spending time on the surface, they spend some of it underground. These five species nest in burrows, which they dig themselves. Most burrows are used year after year.

People and penguins

Like many creatures on Earth, penguins have suffered at the hands of people. The first European explorers to see them killed many for food.

Later encounters were even more disastrous. In 1775 the British explorer Captain James Cook told of large breeding colonies of seals on the beaches of South Georgia in the Falkland Islands. During the next century, hunters killed thousands of elephant seals for the fat in their bodies. Penguins were killed in huge numbers to provide fuel for the boiling pots used to get the fat from

⊙ Penguins do not mind people coming to visit them – as long as they don't get too close.

When people disturb penguin colonies, sheathbills fly in and steal the penguins' eggs. The all-white bird is a sheathbill.

the slaughtered elephant seals. As the seals became scarcer, the penguins themselves were boiled for their fat.

Oil spills

People no longer kill penguins deliberately. Sadly, though, there are many accidental deaths. Oil spillages from ships and leaking pipelines kill tens of thousands of penguins every year. Penguins also suffer when people take too many fish from the ocean, leaving the penguins hungry.

Another problem is the effect of human visitors on breeding penguins. Too many visitors to a colony can cause penguins to desert their nests.

The rarest penguin

The yellow-eyed penguin lives in coastal forests. As people cleared these forests, this penguin became very rare. The places where it lives are now protected and its numbers have increased.

Glossary

colony The place where large numbers of birds come together to lay eggs and raise their young.

crèche A group of young penguins looked after by adults.

crustaceans Tiny animals without a backbone that live in the ocean and form a big part of a penguin's diet.

down A baby bird's soft, warm feathers.

extinct An animal that cannot be found alive anywhere on Earth.

flipper A flat, broad limb that helps a penguin swim through water.

groom To clean and tidy the plumage of another bird.

incubate To sit on eggs to keep them warm, allowing the baby inside to grow.

krill Small shrimp-like crustaceans that live in ocean waters. They are an important source of food for penguins.

moult To change one set of feathers for another. Penguins do it every year.

plumage The feathers that grow on a bird's body.

predator An animal that kills and eats other animals.

regurgitate To vomit up partially digested food. Chicks find this easier to eat than solid food.

squid Fast-moving creatures that live in the ocean. They have tentacles and a torpedo-shaped body.

Further Reading

Books

Bird (Eyewitness Expert). David Burnie. London: Dorling Kindersley/Natural History Museum, 2008.

Emperor Penguins. Deborah Lock. London: Dorling Kindersley, 2011.

I Wonder Why Penguins Can't Fly. Pat Jacobs. London: Kingfisher, 2011.

Penguins. Emily Bone. London: Usborne, 2009.

Penguins! Anne Schreiber. Washington D.C.: National Geographic, 2009.

Rookery of Penguins. Richard and Louise Spilsbury. London: Heinemann Library, 2004.

World of Animals. Susannah Davidson. London: Usborne, 2013.

Websites

Penguins
Information on different kinds of penguins and their lifestyles; with frequently asked questions.
http://edtech.kennesaw.edu/web/penguin/html

Emperor Penguins
Lifestyle and habitats of emperor penguins.
http://animals.nationalgeographic.co.uk/animals/birds/emperor-penguin

Yellow-eyed Penguin Trust
Facts and figures about this rare penguin.
http://yellow-eyedpenguin.org.nz

Antarctica
Information about Antarctica and its wildlife, including some great penguin photographs.
www.antarcticaonline.com

Index